# Dedication

This book is dedicated to my prayer warrior, the woman who taught me, by example, the importance of communicating consistently with our creator through prayer– my Mom. I am forever grateful to have you as a mother. I also acknowledge my dad, Alfred Dunn Sr., who taught me that hard work and dedication will always pay off. To my children: Whitney, Lawanda, Quincy, Quinton, Jazzmine, and Justin, may this be a testimony that you are able to accomplish all things through Christ Jesus who gives you strength. I love you deeply. To all of my grandbabies: William, BreAsia, Aliyah, Moriah, Cerenity, London, Amari, Bentley, Paris, Amir, and Carter Josiah. To my siblings– Angie, Alfred Jr, Rhonda, Kimberly, Michael, Christopher, and TayShawn. May God swing open doors for you that will lead you into divine destiny! I love you all!

# CONTENTS

# Acknowledgement

To God– my Way Maker, Promise Keeper, Mind Regulator, Healer, Provider, and Savior. I never could have done this without you! I acknowledge my grandson Amari Quintez Durrett who spent countless hours with me as I wrote this book. To all of God's Angels that supported me in some way... I thank you!

# Introduction:
# The Steps of a Good Man

**"The steps of a good man are ordered by the Lord, and he delighted in his way!"**
**(Psalms 37:23)**

When I was young, many of us teenage girls would hang around the South Wick neighborhood park in Louisville, Kentucky. We would have good old-fashioned fun playing basketball, singing songs (off key), and competing against one another's step dancing.

We would connect with two or three friends and step dance against the girls from other neighboring communities. Most often, it would be the young girls from the Cotter Homes housing projects or Payton Place. Many days, once our chores were done after school, we would meet to practice our step dances. Each group chose a leader that displayed their ability to lead the team with excellence. This person was the type that loved to dance. They also had to be familiar with all the different dance moves, as well as the music that would be great to dance to. She would strategically plan out what steps and moves we would make. The leader would always come prepared with whatever would be necessary to enhance our ability to learn the steps. She prepared us to be able to dance according to the plan. Oftentimes, she would have the dance routine written down step by step. She would direct whether we would line up two to the left or three to the back and if we would crisscross when we walked out. The leader also took her time to study other girl groups that were popular at the time; Groups like Escape, En Vogue, Oaktown 3.5.7, and of course TLC. We would practice these steps until the street lights came on in our neighborhood. Tirelessly practicing paid off when it was time to compete. For many of the competitions, we took home the victory because *we stepped according to the plan and with perfection.* We were all on one accord following the lead, just as we were told. However, there was a time to my recall that we suffered a defeat. This loss was major. I remember that the crowd was large and our dance team was favored to win. However, we let our fans down. We did not step dance as we had practiced and we lost the competition. As a team, we replayed the mistakes that we had made. We understood that our teammate, whose name was Tracy, had taken a wrong turn and danced off beat. Her inattentiveness was the culprit that took our victory right out from under our feet. As a team, we understood that mistakes are inevitable. This was our lesson from the loss—when your focus is not on the prize, it will cause you to miss opportunities. We had to come to grips with the fact that Tracy wasn't in it to win it. She would often miss practice or she would be preoccupied with other things when she did show up. She didn't pay attention when the leader was teaching new moves. She was easily distracted and would walk according to what her mind was telling her and not according to the plan that was laid out before her. I can also recall that this young lady was very impulsive, hyped, and often had to be redirected. She was told to watch, listen, and learn repeatedly.

That was many years ago and, at my age, I no longer step to the beat of a drum nor compete against steppers. Still, I can't help but extract the principles from the lessons I learned while step dancing. What I found out while being a part of the dance team was that you must step according to the plan that is laid out before you and not according to your own will. This way, you shall do well and the victory shall be yours. Psalms chapter 37 states that "the steps of a good man are ordered by the Lord." This scripture reminded me of the days of my youth: sports, dancing activities, and practicing as a team in order to bring home the victory. In order to get to our destiny, which was the "winner's circle," we had to follow the plans of the leader. My ability to be consciously and physically engaged, as a young girl who desired to be connected to a team, would make an impact within my community– an impact that was very much needed. However, it would be my ability to obey according to the plans of the teacher that would reveal success or failure. The grace of God has given me the chance to be a born again believer– to be a student that may fall, but is completely willing to dust my knees off and get back up again. He has also given me a chance to be a student that is willing to step according to the Master's plan. It is no longer about competing against flesh and blood, but in fact, contending with the faith and completing the race that is laid out before me. Now days, the steps that I shall take are ordered by the Teacher, Jehovah God. These steps are strategic, intentional, and purposeful. When walking according to His plans, I will live a "set free" and victorious life. There is a strategic plan that God has set out for us to be victorious and we must *stick to the plan*. There is no time for us to be deterred and distracted by the mere scrapings of this life. There is no time to second guess the divine steps of God. Make your calling and election sure. If God be God, then believe in His Word and move according to His plan. Proverbs 14:12 states, "There is a way that appears to be right, but in the end it leads to death." God has a strategic plan for all of our lives. In order to be successful in all that we do, we must follow His plans.

"For I know the plans I have for you," declares the LORD, plans to prosper you and not to harm you, plans to give you hope and a future" (Jeremiah 29:11).

Many people often say that life doesn't come with a manual and that life is only what you make of it. However, I beg to differ because God made sure that we would have a manual to follow so that we would one day live a life that would get us to the "winner's circle." Of course, we are all striving to hear God say, "Well done my good and faithful servant." Until then, winning in the *now* consists of being free in our mind, body, and soul. To "win" simply means that you are successful or victorious in a contest or a conflict. We must understand that there is a war going on in our members; a fight between the spirit and the flesh. In this fight, the enemy is out to rob, steal, kill, and destroy. He doesn't play fair at all! The good news is that he is already a defeated foe. The fight is fixed and God has already given us the victory. However, we must tap into the truth of God's Word in order to walk it out.

We win when we are no longer in bondage to man and all the mess! We win when we educate, elevate, evolve, inspire, and endure in the midst of adversity. We win when life says no, but our unshakeable faith says *yes*. We win when we rise above what the naysayers, the doubters, and the haters believe about us. We win when the situation we had to work with was a disadvantage; but we beat the odds, made it work, and prevailed above the competitors. We win when divorce disrupts the entire family structure, but we still manage to live a productive and prosperous life. We win when the doctor's report came back unfavorable but our relentless faith in Jehovah-Rapha (the God that heals) shows up with healing in His wings.

There is a predestined place that He has planned for us to obtain and operate in the "now" and that is "now faith!" The journey before us demands faith that is focused on a God-ordained future. Stepping into divine destiny means moving forward according to the plan of God. On this journey, we are equipped with His power, wisdom, and knowledge in order to be effective in the pursuit of the preordained and predestined plan that was divinely constructed and orchestrated by God. As we progress forward in this life, reaching and pressing onward for the prize of the high calling; our destiny lies ahead of us, not behind.

God's Word is filled with principles and strategic steps that will lead you into divine destinations— if applied correctly. These steps will propel you into a place of spiritual, mental, and emotional prosperity. It is a myth to believe that successful destiny steps are measured by the material things that an individual gains from this life. Things such as money, prominence, fame and power. In fact, the scripture asks a question: "What good is it for someone to gain the whole world, but lose your own soul?" (Mark 8:36).

Many people believe that if they pursue tangible things, it will bring them happiness or fulfillment. However, happiness is not so much about the material things that this life may possess as it is the attitude that you have about life in generfal. Choose to be happy. Choose to be content in whatsoever state you are in. Would you not agree that success is having the peace of God operating in your life when all hell is breaking loose? Be happy and content in who God called and created you to be—despite what others think you should be. Become satisfied in that which God gifted you to be successful in. Press toward the mark for the higher calling. Be determined to finish strong. Be loyal and persistent while overcoming the obstacles that you face while on this journey. Never give up when times appear to be unbearable. Think back to how you made it over before. God did it back then— what makes you think that He will not do it again?

Many would agree that success in life is loving the Lord God with all of our heart, mind, soul, and strength first. Success is all of this and more. Success in this life includes: adhering to the Word of God, being moved by the spirit of God, and not being bound by the flesh. Destiny is inevitable.

However, your destination is revealed by the successful choices that you make. The Word of God allows us to understand that it is better to be obedient to God, rather than offering up sacrifices. For example, when God sent Samuel to anoint Saul as king over his people, he gave him an assignment to wipe out the Amalekites and destroy everything. God said, "Do not spare anyone." So, Saul set an ambush in the valley against the Amalekites and defeated them. However, he spared Agag the king, the best sheep, oxen, fatlings, lambs, and everything that was good. He was not willing to destroy them entirely. Because of Saul's disobedience, God regretted that he called Saul to power and he rejected him as king. God can call you, but disobedience can cut you.

Saul's disobedience was grounded in his need to be pleasing to people. Destiny steps require you to be obedient to God despite your desire to please others. We must understand that God isn't looking for us to give up that which we can't live without. God desires for us to give up our will and take on His Will. God desires for us to give up all of our wrongs for His right way of living. In the book of Psalms, chapter 51, David cries out to God. Verses 9-10 state: "Blot out all my iniquities and create within me a clean (pure) heart, and renew a right spirit within me." David understood that in order to live the life that God called for him to live he would have to be renewed from the inside out. He knew that his heart was deceitful, and desperately wicked.

In order for us to walk according to the plan of God, we must realize that a heart transplant must take place in our lives. The scriptures reveal that "the heart is deceitfully wicked." To align with the plan of God, we must do as David did and cry out to the Lord asking Him to "create within me a clean heart and renew, within me, a right spirit."

All of us must come to the knowledge that

our hearts need a renewal and that it can only be done through the power of God. Only He can create within us a new heart and only He can give us a spirit to do what is right. God reveals that there are two separate wars within our members— the war of the flesh and the war of the spirit. The victory is given to the one that we empower the most! The fight to die out to our flesh will be a never ending battle. However, because of the power of God woven within us, we are declared *more than a conqueror*. Stand your ground and continue to fight with the good fight of faith which shall give way to the new spirit to rise and be dominant. This new heart promotes healing and pushes forgiveness, compassion, and mercy. The renewed spirit will hold fast to the nature of God; striving to operate in the fruit of the Spirit as the book of Galatians chapter 5 reveals: "But, the fruit of the Spirit is love, joy, peace, forbearance, kindness, goodness, faithfulness, gentleness, and self-control against such things is no law."

This journey isn't easy. With God it is achievable! There will be times when you will not make the mark. There will be times when life comes at you really hard. When these times come, you must demonstrate unshakeable faith. Philippians 4:8 reminds us that thinking on things that are "true, honest, lovely, just, pure, and of good report, virtue and noble," will secure a successful destiny step. We must declare that the works of the enemy are null and void in our lives. Today, we elevate our thinking to grow up and mature in the things that God would have us to be successful in. Stepping into our destiny gives no place for the enemy in the "now." There is no time to waste on riotous reminiscing and the rehashing of old, insignificant things that have no part in where God is taking you. You must become so intentional about casting down every wicked imagination that comes against the Word of God. If the thoughts are not building you up, you have the right to break them down! Remind yourself that you are no longer held to fear, confusion, doubt, and disbelief. His Word released us from the old, undisciplined, and unruly actions and attitudes that we once held on tight to. Old things pass away—behold all things become new. Often, our inner selves are the culprit which continues to pacify and stay comfortable with pain that should have been released many moons ago. Did you know that everything has an expiration date to it? Yes, especially outdated pain! It's now time to release the handcuffs off that mediocre mindset. Release that depressed and cantankerous mentality. Let it go. Step into destiny! Declare today that a shift is taking place in your head, and that this shift will no longer allow that old way of thinking to take you out of step. No longer will you hold on to that conception of clutter. Today, you're getting back in alignment with what God has declared for your life. You shall move forward to your divine destiny.

"Brothers and sisters, I do not consider myself yet to have taken hold of it. But one thing I do: Forgetting what is behind and straining toward what is ahead." (Philippians 3:13)

As we step into this God ordained journey, we're no longer held to the captivity of an imperfect past, a difficult present, or a grim future. According to II Corinthians 5:17, we are new creatures in Christ. All the old things are passed away, and everything becomes new. Destiny steps liberate, restore, rejuvenate, and reclaim what's rightfully ours.

The Scripture reminds us that: "the steps of a good man are ordered by the Lord" (Psalm 37:23). Our initial reaction would perhaps be to think that we are not good enough because of the bad choices that we have made in our lives. However, let me remind you of what God said about that which He created...

"...and God saw everything that he had made, and behold it was very good." (Genesis 1:31)

Everything God created was and is good– including you. Of course, we all have room for growth and room for improvement. From the beginning, we were formed and designed *with* greatness *by* the greatest that shall ever live. God created us so well that He gave us dominion and power over all that He created in the earth. From the start, we were created to be the head and not the tail. God blessed and approved us from the beginning of time. We are not a mistake. God loves us so much that He created us with a purpose and a plan. We were on His mind before the world existed.

The Gospel is the power of God. This provides salvation for all who believe. There is only one perfect being and that is God. Paul spoke in the book of Ephesians, "I run this race with patience, nevertheless I purposely let go of things that are behind me and press towards the mark of the high calling which is Christ Jesus."

This journey we call life has a start and a finish point. Although the God that we serve is perfect, the race that is set before us will consist of life's obstacles. At times, we will have negative experiences. No one is exempt from the ups and downs of life. God never promised that there wouldn't be trials. He never promised life would be a bed of roses. He did promise that He would never leave or forsake us. He promised that He would be a very present help in the time of trouble. In this race, there will be times when you pick up speed in order to advance onward. The persistency in your push will give you the power to endure and bring home the victory. Stay humble and never get prideful or pumped up; but do stay the course and keep the promises of God in the forefront of your mind.

There is a prize to compete and contend for. You're not competing against flesh and blood; your battle is with principalities and spirits which live in high places. The slew-footed Devil himself will pull out every wicked and evil device possible in an attempt to deter and discourage you from staying in the race. Nevertheless, these are the moments that you bear down, push, and hold fast to God's promises.

As I consider people in the Bible who persistently pushed their way into purpose, several individuals come to mind. The woman that was harassed with an issue of blood for 12 years *persistently* sought out ways to be healed. The Bible lets us know that she spent all her time and resources in an attempt to find healing. This woman had taken many steps in the wrong direction. Due to wasted time and energy, her condition worsened. Therefore, she was no longer able to stand on her own two feet. She, in fact, became broke down, bent over, and was dragging the ground. This woman was at her lowest point in life. She had no money, no one to help, and was shown no mercy from her own people. However, she made it up in her mind to continue pushing– despite what they said she could not do. She was determined to be delivered! You see, when opportunity arises, you must seize it! This woman was not moved by the crowd that surrounded Jesus. Her focus was on the cure! She strategically set her mind on Jehovah-Rapha, believing that healing was in the hem of His garment. She had the opportunity to get into His presence. She used every fiber within her to push her way until she could no longer physically push! This woman knew it was impossible to touch the hem of Jesus's garment. She still thought: "If I could just touch the hem of his garment, I would be made whole." Because of her grain of mustard seed faith, this woman received healing from Jesus.

There was also a widowed woman who persistently went to a judge for help; she was crying out daily for justice to be done. The judge declared that he didn't believe in her God, nor had any concern for the issue at hand. However, she persistently cried out to him, bothered him, and she pushed until something happened. Despite all the things that were against these two ladies, they had enough confidence in themselves and in their God-given rights to keep on pushing. The Enemy knows his faith; he is a defeated foe and his tactics are to get you to throw in the towel, give up, and drop out. I assure you that God has declared you triumphant— a winner that may not come in first place. You will be triumphant because you stayed the course and finished the race; the prize set before you will be rewarding. The race of the high calling of Jesus Christ affords us an eternal, everlasting, and abundant life; a life free from the bondages of sin. You will fall short of the glory of God, however, the power that lives within you is greater than the external power that you have to control and get back in line. I once heard someone say, "A bird may fly around, and perhaps land in a nest, however, you don't have to let the bird make the nest its home." God has equipped us with the power to resist the Devil, and he shall flee. A mindset that meditates on His Word and a mouth that speaks His Word are the weapons we must use to defeat our flesh.

Sin often feels good, looks good, and smells good. We must understand that the end result is always death or destruction. God already knows the ways that a man shall take. He is not in the dark about our mishaps and or mistakes. Whatever the Enemy means for bad, God will turn it around for our good. God desires for us to grow up and mature so that we can go on to more excellent things.

Adversity is the vehicle that pushes us closer to God. When pain hits us like a ton of bricks, it pushes and provokes us into a position of prayer. Consider the story of Jairus's daughter, who was sick unto death.

"Now, when Jesus returned, a crowd welcomed Him, for they were all expecting him. Then a man named Jairus, a ruler of the synagogue, came and fell at Jesus's feet, pleading with him to come to his house because his only daughter, a girl of about twelve, was dying. As Jesus was on his way, the crowds almost crushed him." (Luke 8:40-42).

If Jairus's daughter had not been suffering with a debilitating disease, he would not have experienced the humble encounter with Christ. His daughter would have gone to an early grave.

God will use our difficult seasons to push us into our destiny. Let's consider the biblical story about Hannah. Elkanah, her husband, loved her more than his second wife Peninah. When it was time to be blessed, he gave Hannah more than Peninah. Hannah was barren and could not give her husband a child. Peninah knew this and began to taunt and tease Hannah. She was dissatisfied with things as they were. The frustration and the insults changed into a desire for more. Hannah was provoked to pray and fast unto God. She went to the temple to cry out to God and to seek His face. God heard her and, in due time, He blessed her with a son called Samuel. One of the greatest prophets that ever lived came out of Hannah's womb because somebody provoked her.

God will make a way of escape from every adverse situation that we shall ever encounter. Know that *nothing* can separate you from the love of God. Because He is Abba, our Father, He is just and faithful to forgive us of our sins and to throw them into the sea of forgetfulness. In order to effectively run the race with endurance, we must acknowledge God in all of our ways and he shall direct our paths. God knows every right and left turn that will lead us into divine destiny; as well as the roads that leads to life's destruction and despair.

He has approved and pre-programmed the GPS– Gods Purposed Steps– so be assured, with confidence that each step possesses the power to propel you into your destiny.

Because your steps are ordered by the Lord, you could very well step into unfamiliar places. These steps are quite different from the obstacles that you may be familiar with from your past experience while running this race. The unfamiliar places consist of new environments, arenas, and ways of life that you've never experienced before. Some of those places may be uncomfortable and out of the norm for you; this is where you must keep in mind that this could very well be the place where you come to know God in a deeper way.

In Genesis chapter 12, The Lord said to Abraham, "Go out from your country, leave your relatives, your father's house, and go to the land that I will show you." Abraham had no clue about where he was going; neither had he been that direction before. With no knowledge of what he would face ahead, Abraham believed the voice of God. He had blind faith, walking by what he knew about God and not by what he would see. God attached promises to his precepts. Abraham had an assignment pinned to his life that would not let him stay around familiar people and places. It moved him into unfamiliar and uncomfortable situations. Abraham answered the call and began stepping into his *divine destiny*. Many times, when God has a purpose attached to his people, He will allow adversity to hit their doorsteps as an attempt to get them moving in His divine direction.

Abraham began to feel the weight from the drought that took place in their community. The crops weren't producing and food was scarce; nevertheless, the famine pushed Abraham to take action immediately. Abraham and his wife packed up what little they had and began taking steps toward the God-ordained destination. Abraham made his way to Egypt and, upon arrival, he was greeted by Pharaoh. Due to his fear, he told his wife Sarai to pretend that she was his sister so that he would not be in danger. Sarai agreed. Pharaoh took Sarai as his own wife, while blessing Abraham with sheep, cattle, donkeys, menservants, maidservants, and camels. Abraham became well off because of the unfamiliar place destiny positioned him in. The story ends with the Pharaoh finding out that Sarai is Abraham's wife. In response, he gave her back to him and allowed them to continue to their next destination. Abraham was able to keep all the things he acquired while there in Egypt. In other words, he did not leave empty handed, in fact, he was blessed going out more abundantly than coming in! (Genesis 12). I believe they both had to trust God in the transition, and their faith in him produced an abundance of provisions that they never imagined. Through it all, they came to know God in a more intimate, up close, and personal way.

Divine destiny steps will position you and I into situations that will promote intimacy with God. For example, we profess that God is our "Jehovah Rapha." How would you know God to be a healer if you've never been sick? What testimony would you be able to share on deliverance if God has not delivered you from anything? Would you be able to let someone know that God is a provider if you've never needed to depend or lean solely on him? Can you truly say that, "God is a keeper," if you've never been kept? Destiny steps will strategically position you to know the power of God in every area of your life. The *transition* (movement) and *transformation* (change) process from what was to what is will cause you to adopt a new perspective about the concept of divine destiny. In that unfamiliar place, you will be exposed to the will of God. The strategic plan of God, although it may not make sense at times, will enhance your ability to become prosperous in all areas of your life.

We must consider the promise that God made to Abraham at a time when he could not see past his circumstances. After Lot separated from him, God said to Abraham, "Open your eyes, look around. Look north, south, east, and west. Everything you see, the whole land spread out before you, I will give to you and your children forever. I'll make your descendants like dust—counting your descendants will be as impossible as counting the dust of the Earth. So—on your feet, get moving! Walk through the country, its length and breadth; I'm giving it all to you." (Genesis 13:14-17)

No one in their right mind registers for a 10-mile race if they have not trained nor have any experience in running long distances. Consider this: God said in Luke 14:28, "For which of you, desiring to build a tower, doesn't first sit down and count the cost, to see if he has enough to complete it?"

We were created with the ability to transform from life unto death. Each stage of our journey has its own ability to push itself into the next stage, shedding what *was* into *what is to become.*

Transformation from the inside out must take place in order to go beyond our present caterpillar state. Consider the principle illustrated in the second chapter of Mark where Jesus spoke: "No one sews a patch of unshrunk cloth on an old garment, otherwise the new patch pulls away from the old cloth, and a worse tear is made. And no one puts new wine into old wineskins, otherwise, the wine will burst, the skins, and the wine is lost as well as the skins. But new wine is for fresh wineskins."

When God has a promise and a plan for our lives, he will position us for the greater purpose.

The condition that God finds us in will eventually go through a metamorphosis stage. He always works from the inside out. He is like the potter with the clay in His hands; working, modeling a masterpiece on the wheel. The potter works from the inside out, much like our Lord. His goal is to craft a new work in the heart, mind, and soul of a person. This is an inside-out job that consists of plucking and pulling out the imperfections. This is a necessary process of becoming the "New Creature." The process doesn't feel good at all, however, it is *good* and *necessary* for divine destiny. Most importantly, it all works out for the good! You can't pursue destiny effectively while hanging on to old habits, old negative thoughts, and old disappointments from folk that let you down. You can't pursue destiny effectively while hanging onto abandonment from folk that walked out on you and left you for dead. "The now" gives you the power to pick up the broken pieces and move forward, allowing the negative situations to be used to empower you to do greater, become greater, and pursue greater! As you pitch your tent and lay your stakes in the way and will of pursuing destiny steps, God will stay just and faithful; He'll keep you in the palms of his hands. He shall hold you up with his right hand, and no situation or circumstance that you face could ever snatch you out of his hands. He will lead and guide you through every step.

Life is evolving; the world continues to turn, even when our lives may feel to be at a standing point. God, who orders the steps of a good person, is always opening doors for us to move forward and walk through. He is consistently enlarging your territory—the closer you get to him.

I'm reminded of the Scripture in Acts chapter 27, where Paul instructed the people that could not swim to grab ahold of the broken pieces in order to get to shore safely. The broken pieces of life have far greater purpose than we can imagine. Choose to take that which was broken and declare that it will no longer carry you *but you will carry it* to get to the other side!

Destiny steps equip you with a plan that will propel you to go deeper so that you can experience the greatness that is within you. The plan God has in place for you is there to give you an expected end. God has laid the foundation for you to grow and build upon while using His principles. His plan is the "Master Plan." He desires for our soul to prosper, grow, and be about Kingdom business. He expects you to win!

We serve a God of order. In the beginning, God strategically created man after his own image. He called the dust of the earth to gather together in order to form the flesh of a man. However, it wasn't until God blew breath into the nostrils of the flesh that the man became a living soul. Adam, the man God created, was given an assignment. God created two of every kind of beast and gave Adam the power to name each of them. God looked upon him after he completed this assignment and noticed that there was no one for him to reproduce with. So, God put Adam into a deep sleep. He opened his chest and strategically removed one of his ribs. God reassembled the rib cage and strategically created a woman suitable for Adam. Then, God gave Adam the privilege to name that which was created for him and, because she came from within him, he declared her as *bone of his bones* and *flesh of his flesh*. She would be called "Woman."

God tactically planned the existence of man. In fact, he created the heavens, earth, and everything within it before he created man. God thought out the process before he moved into his desired direction. This calculated step of God can teach us that, in order to be prosperous, we must acknowledge God's plan in the path that we will take. Our plans and the plans that God has for us are sometimes totally different. God ordained and orchestrated steps will not always be comfortable. We will discuss this in the chapters ahead. However, because He knows the ways that we should take, it shall be well; He shall lead and guide us into all truth.

Take comfort in the fact that the process of change happens in stages. I spoke previously about the transformation that God works in us from the inside out. Consider how this is much like the life cycle or transition of a butterfly. Butterflies go through a life cycle that consists of four stages. The first stage is the positioning of the eggs. This is where the female butterfly lays her eggs onto a leaf. About five days after that, the eggs evolve into the caterpillar.

At this stage, the caterpillar begins to have an enormous appetite, eating and growing constantly. Once it is large enough, it begins preparing for the third stage. This stage is the *chrysalis*—the process of growing from the inside out. This is where the true transformation starts; a transformation that begins internally. The caterpillar will literally eat itself from the inside out. Inside the chrysalis, change is taking place to become the butterfly. The grand finale happens in the fourth stage, where a star is born. A butterfly! A butterfly emerges out of the chrysalis. It can now spread its wings and learn to fly. It can also find a mate to lay its own eggs in order for the lifecycle to begin again!

The power to stay strong and endure the transformative phases of life is in the Word of God. The Word provides stamina and strength, enabling you to mount up with wings as eagles, to run and not be weary, and to walk without fainting. The power of the Word of God changes the stony heart into a heart of flesh; granting us the ability to express unconditional love—love that will look past the faults of others and see the true need of salvation, deliverance, and healing. A new heart empowers you to look at the state of someone else that may be less fortunate than you. You will be able to lend a helping hand. You will go the extra mile with someone who is in need of a listening ear. You will speak into their lives while encouraging them to trust, wait, and seek God.

When you tap into what's already been co-signed by the King of Kings and Lord of Lords, nothing will have the power to convince you otherwise. Destiny steps will cause you to know your true value and worth. We all have heard that diamonds are a girl's best friend. It should be noted that, while this is true, rubies were valued eight times more than the diamond in Biblical times. We are worth far more than any jewel that could ever be discovered. This brings me to remind you that affirmation and validation came from God in the very beginning. Both gems are beautiful, but Rubies are not easy to find. Their locations are exclusive. Diamonds can be found anywhere beneath layers of ground and dirt in mines or caves. Diamonds are present in about 35 countries. You can find them in countries such as India, Russia, and South Africa. They are also being manufactured in labs throughout the world. These are synthetic diamonds. This means that they are man-made and created as copycats. They are not genuine. On the other hand, rubies are naturally created under extreme conditions and they are rare. Your identity is undeniable. You were created with the ability to shine like a diamond and to be rich in every area of your life like a ruby.

In Jeremiah 1:5, God says, "Before I formed you in the womb I knew you, before you were born I set you apart; I appointed you as a prophet to the nations."

The blueprint to our purpose was prepared long before we were placed within the womb of our mothers. In fact, God says, "Before the foundations of the world I knew you." God knew all about what He would create before it ever took on a shape, form, or fashion. God knew you when you were just a thought in His mind. Before you were strategically woven, God had a purpose and a plan for you. You may ask, "What is my purpose in this preordained life? What assignment has God given me?" The answer to the questions at hand can certainly be found through prayer. As the scripture reads, "Acknowledge me in all of your ways, and I will direct your path!" Never look outside of yourself to discover your purpose, everything needed to fulfill your purpose is locked up inside of you!

Your destiny has been stamped, preapproved, and predestined by God. In other words, everything that will transpire in your life *has* to take place. Whether it seems to be good or bad, it all shall work out for the good. At times, it may appear that the trials and tests are almost unbearable. Things may not turn out as you thought, causing the enemy to take jabs at your confidence. Some things may die in your life, however, be reminded that it is all a part of the process. When God is in it, death is not final. This is a fact! Consider when Jesus was falsely accused of treason against the Roman emperor. It was unbelief, wickedness, and bogus lies which brought about the crucifixion of our Lord and Savior Jesus. He was not taken by surprise as to what was bound to happen. Remember, in the garden of Gethsemane, God the Father had warned him about all that he was going to go through. He knew that, in order for us to have access to eternal life, he would have to lay down his life for you and I. He wasn't taken by surprise about the pain that he would endure. He was very much aware of the extreme and brutal process. Still, Jesus agreed to it because it was all a part of God's plan. His communication with the Father assured him that death would not be able to hold him captive. The grave would not be his final destination. It would be turned around for the good! Jesus agreed with the steps that God had ordained. He knew that stepping into the right direction mentally, emotionally, and physically would bring about liberation to those who would believe. He knew that the steps were necessary, divine, and part of the plan of God. The resurrection of Jesus reassures us this—that whatever the enemy may come with, whatever weapon he chooses to harass you with, whatever situation he brings about in order to bring you down—it will all be defeated. Jesus defeated the lies of man, defeated the man-made weapons of mass destruction, *and* defeated death. You, too, have the same power to shake it off, rise up, and move forward. You are a child of the Most High God, and no weapon formed against you shall be able to prosper. Every tongue that rises up against you, every lie, every evil spoken word, and every character assassination attempt—God will condemn them. Step into that divine place declaring, "I shall live and not die!" Declare awakening and resuscitation to the God-given visions and dreams.

Nothing is impossible with God. The promises of God are still *yes* and *amen*. Destiny steps will take you back to the place where you laid your visions down. The places where the enemy stated that you will never be good enough or that you could never accomplish anything in life worth pursuing. The place where you gave up, threw in the towel, and asked yourself, "What is the use in even trying?"

Remembrance is not designed for you to dance with yesterday. It is designed for you to pick up the part of you that has promise attached to it— and to move forward.

He that has begun a good work in you shall complete it 'till the end and that is a promise of God! Shoot for the stars. The sky's the limit. With God on your side, nothing is impossible for you. You can do all things through Christ Jesus which provides you the strength in each destiny step.

In the book of Ezekiel 37:1-6, the Lord took the prophet to the valley, a dry place, and he set him down in the middle of the valley. In the middle of the valley were many dry bones and corpses. God said to the prophet; "Can these dry bones live?"

The prophet replied, "Lord God, only you know."

And the Lord said to him, "Prophesy concerning these bones and say to them: Dry bones, hear the Word of the Lord!"

This is what the Lord says to the bones: "I will cause breath to enter you, and you will live. I will put tendons on you, make flesh grow on you, and cover you with skin. I will put breath in you so that you come to life. Then you will know that I am the Lord."

Destiny steps will position you, front and center, amid a barren and lifeless situation that has caused you to lay down your dreams and visions. A place where what you envision is surrounded by lifeless, dead things. However, at the right time, God will empower you to speak a word. You shall speak words that will shake up the very foundation of that which has been held hostage far too long. The Lord will give the vision life. The breath of God gives us the ability to move forward with all power and might. As you discipline yourself to meditate on and internalize the Word of the Lord, it shall breathe fresh wind upon every godly dream, vision, and idea—calling it forth out of the dust and grave of these earthen vessels. "Lazarus comes forth." The call to that which was declared dead now has life in order to become what God intended.

In the beginning of time, God spoke this world into existence. When He said *let there be light* it became and God declared it to be good. God gave us the same power to create the atmosphere of our lives. Our words are powerful and they influence the course of our lives, so speak life over that which you desire to come to pass. Our words are formed by our belief. In order for us to speak life, we must believe in our hearts. We must have faith that—the God that is able to do exceedingly above all that we can imagine or think—shall make good on his promise. I shall have what I speak! The promises of God are *yes* and *amen.* Step into your destiny, prophesying the Word of the Lord over the journey that is laid before you. In doing so, atmospheres will shift and you will experience a shaking and rattling that produces and releases divine purpose and power. Declare and decree the promises of God over your life and, with faith, they shall come to pass. Push and press forward from the dust of life's disappointments. Release your mind, body, and spirit from the rags and wrappings that came from people that weren't right for you. Breathe. You have been liberated to love, laugh, and live again. Move forward because destiny is waiting on your arrival. Better is in front of you.

Now is the time to declare that you are the head and not the tail. You are above and not beneath. You shall move forward and leave the past behind. God is equipping the Sons, Daughters, Kings, and Queens with divine purpose that will cause us to rise up and go forth. Destiny is calling for YOU!

This study guide will propel you into uncharted land, territory, and places that you have yet to conquer *mentally, spiritually, and emotionally.* The way has already been made. The doors have been opened. The clock has been set. God has given you the permission to pursue and the grace to get going. Now STEP!

You have been divinely chosen to carry out, complete, and conquer the assignment. No longer will you come up with any excuses. If God wanted your spouse, siblings, or friends to do it, he would have chosen them. You have been called and chosen to get the job done. God, who is your shepherd and your source, will provide all that is needed and necessary to carry the assignment out.

In the book 1 Samuel 17:29-52, you'll read the story of David and Goliath. David was the youngest son of eight and he spent his time fighting off the bears and lions that would threaten the sheep. Three of his older brothers spent 40 days on the battlefield, waiting for someone to go up against Goliath the giant.

King Saul made a promise that whomever would take on this Giant would be generously rewarded. So, David took on the assignment of going up against a giant that had everyone walking around afraid. Saul offered to give David his armor. However, David declined his offer and went before the giant with what he had in his possession.

David had a relationship with God. David had five smooth stones and a pocket purse. David went in the name of the Lord and with the strength of the Lord. David took one of the smooth stones and hit that uncircumcised giant right in the center of his head, sending him falling to the ground dead. David then used that which the giant came against him with, his sword, to cut off the giant's head.

Destiny steps take you into the battle knowing that—no matter how big the giant may be—if God be for you, then He is more than that uncircumcised enemy that dares to come against you.

Your confidence is in the spoken Word of God. It has the power to bring down the giant of all giants. Every giant that attempts to disrupt you, your peace, and your divine destiny must bow down at the name of Jesus. Saul attempted to persuade David to wear his armor when he saw that the enemy was heavily suited up. However, because David did not want to appear to be arrogant or rude, he put Saul's armor on—only to quickly take it off while letting Saul know that "his armor had not been proven!" In other words, he thought: *I can't use what you got, I have to use what I have.* That is a lesson for all to learn. Destiny steps will always reveal that which God has placed inside of you—that which will defeat the giants you will face while on this journey. You must be vigilant about using what is inside you! David's refusal to use another man's materials and his faith in what God gave him afforded him the victory over Goliath the giant. I cannot reiterate this enough. I will repeat this over and over again. David knew that he could not lose with that which God had purposed, prepared, and planned for him.

You must be determined not to use that which someone else has been gifted with. Use what you have in your hand that will leave your signature. Never use another person's armor to fight the battles that this life will bring. Yes, it's quite alright to learn from other's strategies that have worked for their success. However, pull from within the God-given treasures you possess, so that your stone will leave the imprint in the head of that giant. David, the mighty man of God, relied on his destiny to dictate his decision to trust God and go up against that which was disrupting the peace of his people. That step blessed everything that he was connected to! Please know that your obedience to the revelation of God will make you able to do all things through Christ Jesus which gives you the strength. Divine destiny steps always carry benefits. God said it best when he said, "Everything that the locust, cankerworm, caterpillar, and the palmerworm has eaten, God will restore everything back unto you. Step into destiny!" (Joel 2:25)

God-ordained steps are not impulsive. In fact, these steps must be strategic plans that have been consciously thought out. God reminds us that we must count up the cost before we began to build anything. Destiny steps will not have you fighting the wind or aimlessly shooting a target that you will never hit. Prepared plans will execute and alienate anything that is out to hinder the progress of God for your life. Planning and preparation prevents many problems. Consider the first chapter in the book of Joshua. Joshua instructed the people to consecrate themselves for the journey (preparation) because in three days (plan) they were going to crossover that which stood between their destinies. Joshua made a declaration— "We are going to cross this Jordan River!" However, it would only happen after the consecration process. Joshua understood the principle of releasing the old in order to receive the new. He was very much aware that—in order to go on to the next level—all things that were insignificant, could bring about doubt, or could hinder the move of God *had* to be left behind. He knew the importance of freeing himself of things that really had no place in where God was taking him to. Joshua knew that they all had to make a sacrifice and let go of some things in order to go higher.

When we hear the word "consecrate" immediately the spiritual discipline called fasting comes to mind. Fasting is simply choosing to give up something that you need or value for an extended period of time. It is the process of dying out to the cravings of the flesh. Let's consider the statement Paul made in I Corinthians 15:31. He said *I die daily.* Paul was simply saying that no longer will he be led by his flesh but, in fact, his will is dead and he shall walk in the spirit of God. *I die daily* states that *I give up what I desire for a far greater glory from the Lord.* Walking into your destiny will require denial of the flesh and a dying out to your will. In order to walk into your destiny effectively, you must adopt this spiritual discipline of fasting. At least once or perhaps twice a week "push the plate back," turn the television off, take a break from social media, and lay yourself upon the altar. If you have the power of the Holy Spirit living on the inside of you, then you have the ability to lay aside every sin and weight. You have the power to break free from the strongholds that so easily beset you! Jesus has already paid the price for you to be loosened from the captivity of the enemy. However, we must have a made-up mind to follow after the will of God. If you have been raised with Christ, then you are dead to the things of the world. You have a new life in Christ Jesus. The old irrational thinking, undisciplined, cantankerous, confused person has died. The life you were once in bondage to no longer has power over you. You've been washed in the blood and set free to step into your destiny. It is very important to apply the spiritual discipline of fasting on a weekly basis. Consecration pushes you closer to God; it allows you to hear the voice that will clarify your purpose and it will empower you to know which way to take. This part of walking into your destiny is important to the assignment at hand. In this world in which we live, everything is fighting for our attention. The focus of our attention must push us to prepare for the greater things that God has in store for us to do and become. Distractions are inevitable. It will happen. As the old saying goes, "A bird may fly over the nest, however you do not have to let the bird find rest upon the nest." In other words, move quickly past the distractions of life. Do not allow the pretty, inexpensive, and cheap wrappings of a lethargic life distract you from moving forward into your divine destiny. The devil will strategically present distractions that will look good on the outside. However, if it's not impacting you to move forward into divine destiny—put it, and them, away!

# Destiny Step #1: Identity

Since the beginning of time, God has had a plan and purpose for all that he created. Everything God has done in His redemptive work is about you and me. We must understand that God created, wove, and fashioned us together to fulfill that purpose. It's interesting to know that He created us all without using the same mold. He made each of us uniquely different. God was so strategic with his creations that no two people possess the same fingerprints. Out of the billions of people in the world, only God could do such a thing so phenomenal. In a world where there are so many people, different nationalities, cultures, and races; you may wonder *where do I fit it in.* You may have asked the questions: "Who am I?" and "Why am I here?" First and foremost, it is very important to know that we all were created after the image and likeness of God. It's important to know that, although a man and a woman were used to carry the seed of a man, we are still the sons and daughters of God. Owning your identity, taking responsibility of who you are, and utilizing the gifts that God has given you will equip you with the power to stand and conquer whatsoever the enemy plans to bring your way. When you know who you are and you stop comparing yourself to others—you are a winner, you are a boss, and you are ready to step into your destiny! Many people waste time trying to imitate someone who God never created them to be. I often ask the question: "Who and *what* stole your identity?" What is it that makes you abandon who you are to take on someone else's identity? When did you lose who God created you to be? In most cases, I've found that peoples' answers include thoughts like: *I wasn't pretty enough*, *I'm not smart enough*, or *I'm not talented enough*. One could say that negativity is expected due to the environment that they grew up in. Maybe they came from a dysfunctional family that was filled with misfits. Or maybe the absence of their mother or father seemingly limited their ability to be great. The negative words spoken into someone's life can prohibit them from loving who God created them to be. It is incidences like these that cause one to change their identity— holding them incarcerated to identity theft. Yes, when you operate under the influence of someone else's identity, you are not living 100 percent to the fullest of who you are. In fact—you, your dreams, your goals, and your greatness are literally incarcerated while you take on someone else's identity. In order to move into divine destiny, you must tap into the greatness of being uniquely you. Everything needed for you to be successful—God has already supplied it.

Greatness lies within your earthly vessel. You must tap into this gift that is destined to do mighty things while on the Earth. Everything God created was good—nothing was missing or lacking when he created you. He designed you perfectly after his image and his image possesses divine purpose!

On the sixth day, He fearfully and wonderfully created man after his likeness and image (Genesis 1; 26-27). He gave dominion, power, and authority to man over everything in the earth.

David writes, "For it was You who created my inward parts; You knit me together in my mother's womb. I will praise You; I have been fearfully and wonderfully made. Your works are wonderful, and I know this very well. My bones were not hidden from You when I was made in secret, when I was formed in the depths of the earth. Your eyes saw me when I was formless; all my days were written in

Your book and planned before a single one of them began." (Psalms 139:13-16)

Throughout the day, there is a powerful dynamic that plays out in our lives that attempts to pervert the promises of God. Because you have been called and chosen to a higher calling, your very existence poses a threat to the enemy's kingdom here on earth. The enemy set out to destroy your divine destiny at an early age—but God knew you, ordained you, and sanctified you before you were a bleep on the ultrasound picture. You were marked as a child of God! When God sanctified you to be great, you were declared unstoppable. Nothing in this world could ever stop you from performing your assignment. The protection of God will confirm it. When Jesus's life was threatened at birth, God informed Jesus's earthly father, Joseph, to rise up and escape from the place that he was in. God told Joseph to do this because the King was out to kill Jesus. God made a way for them to escape.

When you look back over your life, you can see when the enemy tried to snuff you out, tried to kill your dreams, and tried to stop your vision. God made a way for you to escape. Knowing who you are—and knowing what God has declared over your life—should replay in your mind daily. This knowledge is the weapon that will ward off the lies of the enemy. It's not the things that others say about you, it's whatsoever you think about that you become! Proverbs 23 says, "Whatsoever a man thinks in his heart so is he."

It is not about the people that are connected to us. It is not about the history of our past. It is not about our intellect and or education. It is about the beliefs we hold about ourselves that are declared through the *I am* statements that we think about ourselves and speak about ourselves. For example, you could be getting dressed and all of a sudden that still, small voice will harass you: "I am so overweight" or "I'm not smart enough" or "I am not pretty enough." You could be on your job, around someone in a position higher than you, and hear a slight whisper that says, "I am just not good enough. I am too average."

Learn this principle—whatever follows your *I am* statement will always come front and center. You will have that which the mouth speaks. Words hold power. Proverbs 18:21 says, "Life and death are in the power of our tongue."

You are what God created: "fearfully and wonderfully." You are special, distinctively different; the very hairs on your head are numbered. God knows all about you. Stay focused and keep stepping into your destiny! If you believe in God, you can also believe in the power that God invested in you. All things are possible. The enemy will attempt to rob you of your confidence. This is meant to keep you from achieving that which God has already ordained for you to achieve.

In Genesis 29:17, the Bible tells us that "Leah was tender eyed; but Rachel was beautiful and favored." These were two sisters that had the same mother and father; however both had their own identity. The Bible states that Leah was the sister that had a lazy eye. Perhaps, her deformity was unpleasing to look upon, however, that does not take away her purpose of being who God created her to be. Her unpleasant condition prompted people to look at her as "less than" her sister. Because of this, God allowed the deception that her father had orchestrated on Jacob's wedding night. Jacob thought he was marrying Rachel, but in fact he was marrying Leah. To that union, 6 children were born. Leah realized that all she had done for Jacob wasn't enough to win his love. It took having her fourth son to begin to see that the Lord God had favored her. She honored him by naming her son Judah... giving praises to God!

Leah found out that unconditional love could only come from the Father, and that He was due all the praise, honor, and glory. She did make a comment, however, that affords me the opportunity to believe that she was dealing with low self-esteem. She said: "The Lord has noticed my misery, and now my husband will love me (Gen 29:32)." Leah was miserable with her looks, miserable that her husband didn't love her as he should because he wanted her sister who was considered to be prettier. Leah had no confidence in her identity. She had no knowledge of the value she brought to the union. She settled for being number two, while she was technically in the number one spot! She was treated like the other woman although she was the wife. She wasn't in tune with the reality that she had a right to be loved and that she was created beautiful. She was created a queen. Even though she didn't have the features that her sister had, she was still a "diamond in the rough." You may feel that, because you don't look a certain way, you don't measure up to this world's standards of what beauty should look like. Every woman cannot be a size three and we're not all going to have a size 28 waist line. Regardless of your shape or size, know that your inner beauty defines if you're still fine! Speak daily words of affirmation over yourself. What you say shall become that which you desire to see.

You are unique and beautiful just the way God created you to be. Yes—we can all find ways to enhance our beauty— but first and foremost, in order to achieve that goal, we must understand that *we are beautifully made* and the makeup that we apply is simply just an enhancer to my our true, inner beauty. It's not to be confused with the idea that "the makeup makes me who I am." Recognizing our true beauty starts with internally talking to God. Praying unto God and developing yourself with daily declarations and affirmations that will empower you! The power of life and death lies within the tongue so, on this day, speak over your life with words of affirmation! Meditate on these things: "I am the beloved of God! I am accepted and adopted by God. I am a new creature in Christ. All old things pass away and every area of my life will experience the newness of God. I am forgiven for all past, present and future mistakes. I am loved by God, so very much that he has given me the victory over every situation that I will encounter."

Declare and decree that your past will no longer hold you hostage. You are set free to live, love, and laugh. You are blessed in the field and in the city. You are blessed in your down sitting and uprising. You are blessed going out and coming in. You are the head and not the tail. You're the lender and not the borrower. You are highly favored, appointed, and anointed by God. Greater is He that is within you than he that is in the world. You are the light that shines in the midst of darkness. You are a success and everything that God has for you to put your hands upon shall be blessed. Eliminate every negative voice that someone has said about you in an attempt to hold you hostage. Get rid of those lies! Know that you are worthy of honor, worthy of respect, and worthy to be loved just for who you are. You are the apple of God's eye and you are somebody special. Woven within your very being are treasures, gifts, and greatness that is waiting for you to step into destiny. Fan the flames within because you have been chosen to fulfill a preordained purpose.

Love yourself enough to declare, "I love all of me and all of me will genuinely love someone else!" Declare today, "I am destined for greatness because God has declared me as a *good thing!*"

# Destiny Step #2:
# Prayer is Priority!

**"But seek ye first the Kingdom and His righteousness; and all these things shall be added to you." (Matthew 6:33)**

In our quest of walking into divine destiny, God informs us in the Scripture to seek Him and his righteousness first. Everything else will follow. There is power in prayer—it's very dynamic and should not be underestimated. God tells us to pray without ceasing. Jesus revealed to his disciples that men should always pray. Prayer consists of petitioning, thanksgiving, and worship. Prayer is not a time where we just go to God looking for blessings. It's a time for dialogue between yourself and God. When we pray, we're elevated into the realm of the spirit. It is not God coming down to where you are; it is you being elevated to where God resides. Prayer positions you into places that success could never put you in. Most people seek tangible things of this world in order to bring about success, however, true wisdom is seeking the Savior first before you seek success. God told Joshua, "If you take my laws—read, accept, and obey them—you then shall have good success." Seeking God requires constant communication through prayer and studying the Scriptures. Acknowledging God and including him in the decisions that we make and in the situations that we encounter is a form of seeking God. Seeking the Lord throughout our daily lives declares that our will must take the back seat while we allow the will of God to drive us to where we must go. Prayer is essential in living the life that God has planned out for us to live. Prayer is the key to unlocking everything that will ever be needed to carry out the assignment and the purpose that God has given you.

God sent his only begotten Son, Jesus, to fulfill a purpose. Jesus was anointed to preach good news to the poor, to proclaim liberty to the captives, to recover the sight of the blind, to release the oppressed, and to proclaim the year of the Lord's favor. Jesus himself took time to step away and seek the face of God. Jesus knew that prayer is a priority. Our purpose mandates prayer as a priority in our walk into destiny. Scripture reminds us that the sons and daughters of God will be moved by the Spirit of God. For us to effectively operate in destiny steps, the will of God must be the driving force that will lead us into that prepared place of *divine destiny*.

Prayer reverses the curse. In the book of 2 Kings, chapter 20, the Prophet Isaiah went to Hezekiah while on his sick bed with these discouraging words: "Set your house in order, for you shall surely die and not live."

Hezekiah was very ill; he was at the point of death, to be exact. God sent the prophet to let him know that he needed to get things in order. Things like preparing a will and telling the family about his final wishes. However, Hezekiah wasn't quite ready to throw in the towel. I believe Hezekiah knew that his assignments were not done. He wanted to live full and die empty. Upon hearing the awful news, Hezekiah turned his face to the wall and prayed to the Lord. "Remember me Lord!" This is how he started his prayer off—as if God has forgotten him. He reminded the Lord of the things that he had faithfully done to please Him. Hezekiah did what he knew to do in order to touch the heart of God. He earnestly prayed. His prayer came from a sincere heart. His prayer moved the heart of God, causing Him to hear his cry. God saw his tears, answered his prayers, and added 15 more years to his life. Prayer from a sincere heart reaches the heart of God. No matter what the report of man may determine, you can make a conscious decision to step into the realm of faith. With God, all things are possible. As you walk into destiny steps; obstacles, tough situations, sickness, and other unfavorable circumstances will occur. In those moments, be reminded to turn and trust in the Lord with all your heart. Continue to seek Him and rest assured knowing that the strength, mercy, and grace that you need shall be provided. In the book of Philippians 4:6, the Scripture tells us not to be anxious about anything, but to make our petition be known unto God and to pray with supplication and thanksgiving. I know that, when we follow this principal, God is ready and willing to do that which he has preordained to be carried out in our lives. We must be patient and wait upon the Lord. He will cause us to mount up upon wings of eagles; we shall run and not get weary; and we shall walk and not faint. Wait on the Lord.

There's power in prayer—God spoke that the prayers of the righteous avail much. God shall supply all of your needs according to His riches and glory. Simply make your request be made known unto God in prayer and He who is just and faithful will show up on your behalf.

Many of us are not patient; we want what we want—when we want it. Oftentimes, if we are honest, moving too fast has gotten us into situations that we had no business being in. Being impatient and setting out to do what you want to do, instead of what God has planned for you, can cause some painful experiences. Fortunately, we serve a sovereign God that will love us back into alignment with Him. God says, "Let patience have her perfect work." (James 1:4)

Some things must "stew," as big mama said. Let it simmer a while and don't be so quick to move. When the time is right, you will be in the right place at the right time. God makes good on His promises—remember— they are *yes and amen*.

The Kingdom of God is at hand for us to possess. Walking into our destiny will challenge us to transition from what *was* to what *is*. We were created and equipped with power, dominion, and authority to possess each step we take. In other words, own what you tread your foot upon!

There is a quote by Marcus Garvey that says: "A people without the knowledge of their past history, origin, and culture is like a tree without roots." It is very important that you embrace your history, learn from it, and move forward. You must change the memory of your past into a hope for your future. We cannot change our past. We cannot change the fact that people act in a certain way. We cannot change the inevitable. However, we can build on failure and use it as a stepping stone to move forward into that which God has purposed for us to obtain. Whether good or bad, you can use the experiences and mistakes you've made to propel yourself into your prepared future. Don't allow the enemy to trap you into a guilt trip about your past failures. The enemy always haunts you with past failures rather than your past success.

You've done what you've done; now move on. You can't go back and change it, however, you can extract the wisdom from the mistake, move forward, and grow. You cannot fully understand where you're going until you fully understand the test and trials that you've gone through.

God's plan for you involves reaching the Promised Land. Obedience to God and consistent prayer are Kingdom principles that will propel you into it. He has had you on his mind since the foundations of the world. He was fully aware of the flaws that you would possess. He knew about the dysfunctional families, trauma, abuse, neglect, and abandonment that you were going to go through. God knew and still he chose you for the assignment!

God has loved you unconditionally and protected you like no other. God delivered you out of the hands of the enemy, and sent his only Son to shed his blood for you. Who wouldn't set quality time aside to communicate with the one that has given them the very breath of this life? In other words, communication between you and God cannot be put on the back burner. Be mindful that it is in God that we move, live and have our being. We must be committed to being consistent in communicating with our Creator. He must not be treated like a genie in a bottle that can be rubbed and convinced to give us whatever we'd like. No... He is God of the Universe and He is worthy of our time.

In fact, if you and I do not pray to the God that is able to do all things, we will not have the power to carry out any given assignment from God!

It's one thing to appear to have or pretend to have a form of salvation, however, the real power is in being saved. The assignment God has for us to complete first and foremost is to witness to the power of salvation. We are a witness to the reality that the enemy has no power over our lives because God has set us free. We are a witness to the fact that—when we were polluted in our own blood and struggling to live—God rescued us out of the mental madness. It was God and God alone that snatched us out of a sinful, sinking soul. In this season, it's not about being popular. It's about being powerful in the things of God. Prayer is essential to our divine destiny. We must consistently start our day face down, communicating with God through prayer. Thank God for the hope that is within you. Thank God for the hope and knowledge that nothing will be able to separate you from His love. The Father is He who cleaned up your mess and presented you with the message that—*if it had not been for God on my side, where would I be?*"

Don't allow the enemy any access to keep you hostage to your history. Stop apologizing and feeling guilty over that which God has forgiven you. It's done, Now repent and get to stepping! After all that you went through and all that you experienced, you're still in your right mind. You owe God that alone time. It will be the alone time with the Creator that will empower you, strengthen you, and prepare you to be effective, unmovable, and unbothered. Prayer is not a time for you to simply dump all of your wants upon God. He is not a genie. However, He knows what you stand in need of before you even ask! Prayer raises the dead and anything that is lacking oxygen or breath. Prayer delivers you and me out of anything that threatens our purpose. Prayer heals every wound and mends every broken piece. Prayer will cause your enemy to be your footstool. Prayer positions you in places that man said that you could never be. Prayer parts the Red Seas of our lives. Prayer brings recovery, restoration, and salvation to those wayward family members. Prayer will make a wrong situation turn right! Prayer confuses the enemy. Prayer confines the enemy's weapons and convicts his strategies. Prayer is the key to your power! What a mighty God we serve! Condition your mouth to simply say *thank God* for that which you're petitioning him for. Cry out to God, worship him, and declare His name great in the earth.

# Destiny Step #3: Step into Obedience

**"I call heaven and earth to witness against you today, that I have set before you life and death, the blessing and the curse. So, choose life in order that you may live, you and your descendants." (Deuteronomy 30:19)**

There is power in having the ability to make decisions on your own. However, the power of life and death lies within the decisions that you choose to make. God has given you that power to choose. When we choose to move forward in Him, we have chosen to live an abundant life. We have chosen the blessings of God. God sent His only begotten Son,

Jesus. He came that we may have life—and have it more abundantly. What do "steps to obedience" have in common with living an abundant life? Choosing the life that God has planned out for us will provide an abundant life. God is *the Way, the Truth, and the Life.* In order to effectively walk in your destiny; we must have a relationship of obedience with the "Destiny Deliverer!"

Disobedience will always bring about defeat, and depletion. I'm reminded of the disobedience of the children of Israel while they were going through the wilderness. Their disobedience unto God caused them to walk around the same mountain for 40 years. For many, their destiny was to die in the wilderness. Time after time, God showed the people His power. He sent manna down from heaven, water out of a rock, and parted the Red Sea so that they could walk through on dry land. However, instead of having a spirit of thankfulness, they were ungrateful, stiff necked, and still cried out that it was better for them to stay in Egypt (bondage) where they were able to eat the leeks and the onions. These people were set on self-gratification. Never mind the fact that God parted the Red Sea in order for His people to walk out with their families. God gave them more than they'd ever had. With all that God had done, the people still complained. These people had their minds set on a good meal and they wanted it no matter what.

When we make it our priority to sit with the Father, hear His voice, and be moved by His spirit—His word shall be the compass that leads and guides us into all truth. We know that God honors obedience. Obedience is better than anything we could ever offer up as a sacrifice unto the Lord. Our obedience to the will of God will provide a lamp unto our feet. As we step into destiny, every step will be illuminated by the light upon our pathways.

Regardless of our financial status, culture, background, family dysfunction, color, or creed: God has empowered us to move out of *what was* in order to step in to *what is* and what is too come. God said, "Who the Son sets free is free indeed." You have been released from any and every thing that would hold you into bondage. The gag of silence has been taken off of your mouth. Now cry aloud and spare not. Speak! Speak life!

The pain of the past holds limited power over your future. Discipline yourself to meditate on the Word of God and to understand the will of God for your life. Your future is now equipped with God's power to "return to sender" the pain it penetrated within you. The sender is not the person that harmed or inflicted you with pain. It is not the person that abandoned, rejected, misused, or abused you. Remember—we as children of God— are not fighting against one another. The battle we're in isn't against people, but against spirits and principalities in high places. Our fight is to maintain the faith that we have in the written Word of God! Our fight is to die out to our flesh in order that we may have life in Christ Jesus.

In the book of Luke chapter 22, the writer lets us know that it was only after Jesus prayed unto the Father that he agreed, out of obedience, to the set plan of God. Jesus, in the garden of Gethsemane, was approached by his disciple, Judas Iscariot, and an entourage of soldiers. The timing was perfect. They came looking for Jesus in order to start the process of the crucifixion. However, they needed clarity as to who Jesus truly was. Judas decided to grace Jesus with a kiss in order for the soldiers to know who he was. Jesus knew the purpose behind the kiss. He asked Judas the question, not for him to get clarity, but for Judas to be fully aware of what he was doing. Jesus said, "Judas, are you betraying the Son of Man with a kiss?" God has a purpose for everything. Judas began to operate in the wrong spirit, but it was all part of the plan. I believe we must understand that, when it's part of God's plan, even the closest people to us can be used by the enemy to get us to that divine place.

When pain presents itself, we must still choose to be obedient to the process. Obedience can be learned through situations where we suffer. In the case of Judas Iscariot betraying Jesus, he did not know that the betrayal was necessary in fulfilling the plan of God for the Son of Man.

What would you do when someone that has history with you was chosen to hand you over to the enemy? This is someone who spent quality time with you, witnessing the power of God operating in your life and in your ministry. Judas saw the miracles that took place in the lives of the people that were blessed by Jesus. He witnessed the sick, feeble bodies being healed and the lame rising up to walk at the name of Jesus. He saw the eyes of the blind regain their sight. He witnessed the crippled and crazy being clothed in their right mind at the name of Jesus. Judas's purpose had a time and season connected to it. He couldn't do what was planned until God allowed it to take place. God knew that the end of Jesus's purpose here on earth was drawing close, so he allowed the betrayal to take place—at the set time. Judas had no clue that he would be the culprit who would be used to push Jesus into divine destiny. The bible states that, "Satan entered Judas Iscariot, one of the twelve, and then he went to the chief priests and the offices of the temple guard and discussed with them how he might betray Jesus." (Luke 22:3-4)

On a day when Jesus went into the garden to commune with God, the enemy was strategically planning his attack. Jesus prayed so earnestly unto God that great balls of sweat, like blood, fell from his face. God, the Father, had revealed to him what must take place in order for all mankind to have the opportunity to be free from the bondage of sin. He revealed this to Jesus in order for all humanity to have the chance to live a life pleasing to God. God revealed that Jesus must be beaten, broken, and bruised upon the cross. However, it didn't end there. He would raise Jesus from the dead so that we, too, would have the power to be raised from death into eternal life. Knowing what was to come, Jesus continued to be obedient. He spoke to His Father, "Not my will, but let thy will be done."

On this journey to divine destiny, you will encounter people that smile in your face and talk about you behind your back. These can even be individuals that have witnessed the power of God operating in your life. There are people that are waiting for the opportune time to turn you over to the wolves, and to sell you out! However, when that time comes, just know that your obedience to the will of God will cause you to be triumphant and victorious. Nothing the enemy would ever do could take God by surprise. In fact, He knows what's going to take place before it happens, and it shall work out for your good. In the book of Job, the enemy had to get permission from God to vex Job's spirit. He had to kill all of Job's children and destroy everything he owned. There was one thing the enemy couldn't do to Job and that was to take his life.

In those moments when your Judas rises his ugly head in your life, celebrate him. Let him know that he is, in fact, your personal purpose pusher. Judas is going to get you to the divine place of God. Stay humble and obedient.

If, on this divine destiny journey, you have been fortunate to not have experienced the betrayal of a Judas–arm yourself likewise to suffer! Pain comes in all shapes, sizes, colors, and cultures. During this journey, you will be offended. If you're a Christian, you will attract offenses. The enemy is mad at you. Remember, at one time, he lived in heaven–the place of your divine destination.

Don't curse the pain of your past or present, because it propels you into the place where power is magnified. God shall be glorified and the enemy is horrified. The pain equipped you with the power to love those that hate you and say all manner of evil about you. The pain equipped you wth the power to declare and decree the promises of God upon your life. It equipped you with the power to be free from the bondages of sin and the mess of yesterday. It equipped you with the power to be a witness to know that, if God delivered me, He can to deliver you.

Our testimonies of perseverance in the face of the enemy will bring hope to the many who are seeking to stay the course and finish the race. If we had no scars, I truly doubt that we would ever be able to witness effectively to those that we encounter as we step into destiny.

# Destiny Step #4: Time to Step!

In Ephesians 5, Scripture informs us to redeem the time that is before us. In other words, we need to make the most of every opportunity. Redeem the time; take back that which was lost. We must make a conscious decision to recover the time that the enemy has stolen. Be intentional and maximize every moment that you have in your possession.

Time—whether you're black or white, rich or poor—we all have it in common. However, how we spend our time is what shall set us apart. Are you a procrastinator? Are you slothful, slow, and stuck or are you in progression and moving forward? Now is the time to decide how you will spend your time and energy. Remember, NOBODY can redeem wasted time!

Ecclesiastes 3:1 reveals that there is "A time for everything and a season for every activity under the heavens." The right time for everything will produce successful results. Timing is precious and it's valuable. Make every opportunity count. Put your best foot forward. It is never too late for greatness. Don't try to rush things into place because, in doing so, you can experience the weight of the push if you're not moving in God's timing. Destiny steps demand that you operate with the peace of God in your life

Hebrews 12:1 says, "Therefore, since we are surrounded by such a huge crowd of witnesses to the life of faith, let us strip off every weight that slows us down. Let us run, with endurance, the race God has set before us."

In the book of Ecclesiastes, chapter three, God reveals to us that He has a set time for everything under the sun.

In order to move effectively into your destiny, God will allow a season of separation. Time that shall require the uninterrupted chaos of life. This time will reveal your purpose, prepare the plan, build you up, and position you for the promise. This time will progress the purpose of His promises upon your life. In 2 Timothy 1:6, Paul wrote to Timothy telling him to "stir up the gifts that are within you" and to "fan the fire." For God to make that statement, He knew that there would come a time that the fire, or power within us, would burn out or get weakened by the cares of this life. He knew that there would be a time when the gift He blessed us with would take a back seat and wouldn't operate to its full potential. Life and its situations can push us into places that are not designed for us to stay in. For example, the death of a loved one can have such a traumatic effect on one's emotions that it could cause the person to be depressed or saddened to the degree that they just don't feel like doing what they normally would do. Whatever curve balls life brings at any given time can cause "the gifted one" to still away from the routines and the day-to-day activities. This time away from distraction will rekindle the fire and re-flame the coals that are burning within to move you forward into your destiny.

Destiny awaits, purpose is pushing, and the clock upon the wall reads, "Timeout for business with no balance." Say goodbye to being a busybody. Maybe you are a jack of many trades, yet you're mastering none. There is no time for mediocrity or the mundane mess. Yes, there have been times when we have failed. Mistakes and mess-ups have been made, however, every hard knock and hard rock encounter while on this journey shall be used to propel us into the pre-planned purpose for our lives. Remember, David defeated Goliath with a word and a rock. God was with David, and He shall be with you. "All things work together for our good." (Romans 8:28)

Walking into your destiny may mean that you write the book, start the ministry, or announce the call upon your life. Walking into your destiny will allow you to invest in yourself—your dreams, your goals, and that which you are passionate about. Destiny is that which you breathe and are drawn to. God invested in you so much that He gave His only begotten Son, Jesus, to be wounded for your transgressions, to be bruised for your iniquities, and to be chastised for your peace.

Step into destiny. Write the vision—today. Make it clear. Start the business. Explore the world and take that leap into faith as you embrace your destiny steps!

Isaiah 43:19 says, "Behold I will do a new thing, now it springs up, do you not perceive it?"

God is moving those who He has chosen from the old state of being—acting and operating in their old ways—and is ushering them into the newness of who He is and who they are in Him. Your perspective, mindset, desires, atmosphere, intellect, associates, and taste buds will change as you step into your divine destiny. No longer will you be stuck living beneath your purpose. No longer will you entertain or embrace that which you don't see as a part of your future. It is now time to fly with the eagles and soar high above that which you were once familiar with. It is now time to expand the horizons and experience life in a way that you've never done before. For many, it could be as simple as maintaining the joy of the Lord as the new thing, or maintaining healthy relationships with people that are headed in the right direction. In this season, the timing is all about tapping into an area of new things, new places, and new people.

Be determined to use words that are in reference to your preference. Consistently speak toward your future. Intentionally move forward and leave those things behind that don't push you into your purpose. Be unapologetic about who and what you allow to get in your face and speak into your life.

Always be conscious of the voices you allow to infiltrate your ears. Please remember, the enemy speaks smooth, soft words that sound like truth. You must attentively listen with your heart for the word of the Lord. It's very important, on your journey to destiny, to remember that *evil communication corrupts good manners*. The voice of negativity, or the association of a familiar spirit, if allowed, could activate the old man that God delivered you from. You must understand that we must not put any confidence in our flesh! Entertaining familiar spirits can plague your purpose.Know that whatsoever you allow to reign in your life will eventually rule over your life.

Destiny steps push you into a place of influence. Who you connect with does have an effect upon your life. If you're not careful, bad communication can infect you. In this season, attaching yourself to positive people is the new you. You can become guilty by association with negative people. The Bible reveals, "How can two walk together unless they are in agreement?" (Amos 3) Associating with the wrong people is like having two different types of animals—with two different personalities and two separate goals—tied together with a yoke around their neck. They will each struggle to pull the other in its own direction. Understand, there's no time to be pulling or dragging anyone that isn't going in the right direction.

"Nothing that goes in from the outside can defile a person; however, it is that which is on the inside of a person that defiles a man/woman." (Mark 7:15)

On this journey to destiny, keep the Word of God in the forefront of your mind. Guard your heart because the issues of life truly flow out of it. Positive vibes, encouragement, and wisdom are always accepted. After all, your entire goal is to possess the good fruit of the land.

# Destiny Step #5: Stay the Course!

In the book of Exodus, we find that Moses was chosen by God to lead the people of Israel out of captivity by way of the Red Sea. God chose Moses to approach the King with the message: "Let my people go." Pharaoh was rebellious and disobedient to the command of the Lord. The consequences for his behavior brought about many plagues upon his people and even the death of all of their first born sons. Moses led the people out of captivity by way of the Red Sea, however, he was not allowed to go into the Promised Land. God raised up another leader by the name of Joshua. In Joshua chapter 1, God gives Joshua specific instructions that pertain to being a successful and prosperous leader. He revealed that wherever Joshua would plant his feet—that land would be given to him. This promise was spoken by God before the journey began. He also made it clear that Joshua should be strong and very courageous. He explained that Joshua should not depart from the book of the law and that it should always be in his mouth and on his mind.

He told Joshua to meditate upon it and "not to turn to the right hand or the left." In other words—God was telling Joshua to keep his mind upon Him, for it is the Lord that will keep you in perfect peace. God revealed to Joshua that his way shall be prosperous, and he shall have good success by doing what God instructs him to do.

God also spoke to Joshua, "Every step that the soles of your feet shall tread upon, it's already yours." God chose him for the assignment. He gave him the assurance that—wherever he set his foot—the territory would be given unto him. God is no respecter of persons. What He has declared for one, He can do for another. Stepping into your destiny to advance the Kingdom of God consists of you having total access to every place that the soles of your feet shall tread upon. You, too, have purpose that is attached to a preordained assignment. God chose and equipped you to handle everything that will transpire while on this journey. God has given us the necessary equipment to make it through. Trusting the Word of God and relying upon His will and His way will cause us to be successful and prosperous in the role or leadership position that God has called us to. Yes, there will be a time in our lives when we will get discouraged and feel that there is no support from people that we depend on. Even in those moments, you must began to encourage yourself. Speak over your life that you shall possess the land. You are more than a conqueror and God has declared you triumphant.

God would have you to use your voice to decree and declare that any spirit that would try to hinder you from moving forward is null and void—in the name of Jesus. It is your voice that will change, liberate, and proclaim the Glory of God!

Only the steps of a good man or woman are ordered by the Lord and, where He guides, He shall provide.

Effectively walking into destiny will cause unexplained and unexpected doors to open for you. The path that God has planned for your life has purpose attached to it. God will give you strategies and solutions to the issues that you face in this life.

In Luke 8:43-48, the story of the woman with the issue of blood reveals that she had a life issue. In order for anyone to be deemed a living soul, they must have blood flowing through their veins. This woman had a blood issue seeping out from within her and no physician was able to heal her. This was a job for Jesus—and him alone. We must not turn up our nose to this woman who was bleeding all over the place. You may never have a blood issue to the extent that she had, however, you shall experience the nasty, foul, and almost unbearable issues that life has to offer. Having unwavering faith in God to work out those issues will always manifest His deliverance power. When we call on Jesus, the Son who came to set the captives free, no issue that you and I could ever encounter will be able to keep us bound. There shall be new innovations, ideas, and visions as you walk out your destiny steps. Every forward step you take will advance and transform the Kingdom. So it is in heaven, it shall be on the earth.

God is the same yesterday, today, and forever. He is no respecter of persons. What he has done for one of His children, He will do the same for another.

Destiny steps focus on what's ahead, regardless of what has been left behind. Keep your eyes upon the author and the finisher of your faith. In doing so, each destiny step you take will equip you with the power to overcome every obstacle that you will face. Keep in mind that if you don't faint, you shall reap what God has in store for you. Remember, it is in God that we live, move, and have our being. The disappointments of this life cannot compare with the things that God has in store for us. I heard someone say, "Take the lemons life hands you and make lemonade." Regardless of how you look at your situation, God has called you to arise and move out because your destiny is calling. "All things are working out for your good."

# Destiny Step #6:
# You are an Overcomer

**"These things I have spoken to you, so that in me you may have peace in the world you have tribulation but take courage; I have overcome the world." (John 16:33)**

There is power through the shed blood of Jesus Christ. Your faith in God equips you with the power to overcome every issue and obstacle that you could ever encounter in this life. Jesus himself was tempted in all ways, yet He was still without sin. He overcame the insults of man, the lies of the enemy, the wounds of wretchedness, and the death of the cross. Low self-esteem, neglect, abuse, abandonment, rejection, guilt, lies, and defamation of character was nailed to the Cross. Jesus resurrected from the grave and so shall you!

The internal voice screams louder than the external voice. It's not what someone else has spoken in your life—it's what you believe within yourself. God reveals to us that "all things are possible if we believe." For many of us, it's been a struggle to rise up from the venom of evil words that were spoken over our lives. For many, the words wounded you to the core, leaving you somewhat paralyzed, emasculated, and crippled. Hurt people hurt other people. It is now time to rise above the lies that the enemy has spoken. You must declare that those words will not rob, steal, kill, and destroy you. Yes, the dark areas may exist, but you must command every word to be cast out. Command that every spirit that comes to oppose the will, plan, and hand of God upon your life will not shut you down mentally, spiritually, emotionally or intellectually.

Speak the Word of the Lord over your life and watch it manifest His glory. It will be the words that you speak over yourself, and speak into the atmosphere, that will bring about a powerful transformation. Spend quality time with the Lord, meditating on His word to the degree that seeds are planted within your heart. He has already given us the power to come boldly to the throne of God. Sowing your time in the Word equips you with power to cast down every lie that the enemy comes to rob, steal, and kill your purpose with. The harvest you shall reap will be life, and life more abundant. Arise, and combat the lies of the enemy! You have the authority. Man or woman up! Your ammunition is the Word of God! Use it to assassinate that which is attempting to take you out of your destiny. This step is "kill or be killed." Destiny steps never lay down their weapons. We're suited up with the Armor of God. The armor is the breastplate of righteousness, the sword in our hand, and our feet prepared for peace.

In the book of Joshua, God instructed the people to walk around the wall of Jericho for seven days. On the seventh day, the people walked around the wall seven times and then they were ordered to open up their mouth and shout. In doing so, the wall of Jericho went tumbling down. Just like these people, you have the victory. It lives within you.

Walking into your destiny dares to be different. You are unique and have been set apart for Kingdom purposes. Destiny walks in determination and not defeat. Your purpose always progresses to a greater level, despite the giants that occupy the territory.

Looking at the book of Numbers, chapter 13, the Lord told Moses to send men to spy out the land of Canaan, which God was giving to the children of Israel. Moses sent one man from each of the 12 tribes. The 12 men went up before the people and surveyed the land. The report brought back by the group explained, "We went to the land where you sent us, it truly flows with milk, and honey."

Destiny tip: *The enemy will always present some truth, followed by a lie.* He is the father of lies. Anything spoken contrary to God's word is a lie from the pit of hell.

The group continued to describe their findings: "Despite God's faithful promise, the people who dwell in the land are strong. The cities are fortified and very large. We saw the giants in the land, and we are as grasshoppers in our own sight."

Another destiny tip: *See yourself through the lenses of God, not the eye lashes of man.*

The negative report brought back by the 10 spies caused an entire community of people to become fearful and doubtful. The low self-esteem they possessed was branded on the hearts of the others. Upon seeing the giants, the mentality of the ten spies was defeated.

However, the report of Joshua and Caleb was different. They reported back: "We are well capable of obtaining the promise of God and we can take the land." These two knew that, with God, nothing would be impossible.

Destiny steps require surrounding yourself with some Joshuas and Calebs. Surround yourself with folk that are not afraid to do what is necessary to possess the Promised Land. If God spoke destiny into your spirit—believe God. Guard your ears; place a gate over them against anything spoken contrary to the Word of God. Whenever you hear the words *you can't*, always remember that God said, "You can do all things through Christ which strengthens you" (Philippians 4:13).

# Destiny Step #7:
## Believe that His promises are *yes and Amen*!

We all, at some time or another, have been let down by someone in our life. We've all have experienced being lied to. However, this isn't the case when it comes to God making a promise to us. When God makes a promise, he makes good on it. He lets us know that his promises are *yes and amen.* God says that just a small seed of faith—as small as a mustard seed—would move mountains. Now we know that mountains are fixed on a strong foundation, of course until something traumatic such as an earthquake, or shifting in the foundation takes place. However at any moment the cares of this life could weigh heavily upon you as though someone picked up the mountain and sat it right onto your lap! And in the midst of it, your ability to draw strength from your faith taking confidence in the unwavering promises of God will cause that mountain to be removed in Jesus's name !

God had clearly promised the land to the children of Israel, but their problem was that they didn't believe. The people dealt with low self-esteem and a lack of faith. The perception of the giants being large could have very well been true, however, they failed to remember that even the giants were subject to Gods power. They negated the fact that nothing is too large or hard for HIM.

The victory was in the spoken word—despite the giants that were before them. Their doubtful response was a potent combination of truth, lies, and exaggeration. It was true from a human's perspective; the giants were stronger than them. "We are not able to go up against the people," that of course was a lie. It was contrary to what God had already spoken. Their problem was clearly a lack of faith in what God had spoken. The people were unaware that it is God that holds the plans for their life, and in His plans he provides an expected end that declares you and I as victorious!

You have the victory over every battle. Remember, the battle does not belong to you—it belongs to the Lord. It is in the will of God for the territory He has declared yours to be confiscated by you. God said that He will give you wells that you did not dig, and land that you did not purchase. If God said it, that settles it. Your faith is fixed on His word. You're not walking by what you see; you're walking by what you know to be true in God!

Expect to cross over into the Promised Land. That half of the battle is already won. Simplify your life. All you need is one, two, or three believers coming together; touching upon anything on this earth, and you will find God front and center in the midst of your prayers. Our God is able to deliver us from this diminishing, deteriorating world. He is able to keep us from the harm of all of our enemies. Nothing is too hard for the God that you serve. The giant that stands before you is minute compared to the great God that you have fighting on your behalf.

Ask yourself: "If God be for you, who can be against you" (Psalms 91:7)?

For some of you, the steps of the uncharted terrain will require crazy faith. God would not give you orders to move out if He wasn't going to make a way in the desert for you.

"Because he has set his love upon me, therefore I will deliver him. I will set him on high, because he has known my name. He shall call upon me, and I will answer him; I will be with him in trouble; I will deliver him and honor him. With long life I will satisfy him and show him my salvation" (Psalm 91:14-16)

Remove all that is unimportant and focus on your dreams and goals.

"Keep your mind stayed upon Him, and he will keep you in perfect peace." (Isaiah 26:3).

Scripture informs us to acknowledge God in all of our ways, and he will lead us into all truth. Destiny steps require for us to be mindful that God is omnipresent. He is forever present and He knows all things. Our minds must be fixed upon his Word and every wicked, high-minded imagination must be cast down. We are to think on the things that are lovely, pure, just, noble, and praiseworthy. In other words—think positive and be Kingdom-minded. To move forward effectively, we must train our minds to trust God.

God desires for you to operate with a Kingdom mentality while here on earth. We must aim to go higher in our thinking. We can't be comfortable in a tight place. God designed you and I to operate in a place of greatness! Our mentality must conquer a new territory. God desires for us to live an abundant life. He shall stretch, and challenge us into an arena that promotes inner growth and external victories in our every step. Destiny Steps expand, and enlarges our territory! There's more living on the inside of you! You have the capacity for overflow!! Elevate up, sky is the limit!

Of course on this journey obstacles are inevitable. However these shall be opportunities for God to show himself strong. God declares that many shall be the afflictions of the righteous—however, be assured that the Lord shall deliver you out of them all (Psalms 34:19). Trouble will come, but the Lord is your Shepherd and you shall not stand in the need of anything. Harness the confidence that God has invested within you. God is supplying all the strength that is needed for you to finish the assignment strong. Just be reminded that the obstacles are simply challenges that pushes the greater change in you that shall manifest.He loves you so that God will not let you stay average when He created you for greater.

Isaiah 41:10 reminds us not to be fearful, because God is with us, and do not dismayed; for He is our God. He will strengthen, help, and uphold us with His right hand of righteousness.

# Destiny Step #8: P.U.S.H
# (Press Until Something Happens)

In the book of Exodus, chapter 1, King Pharaoh called the midwives into his office with this order: "When you help the Hebrew women give birth, observe them as they deliver. If the child is a son, kill him, but if it's a daughter, she may live." However, the midwives feared God and did not do as the king of Egypt had told them; they let the boys live. When Pharaoh found out that the women went against his orders, he was furious and had the midwives—Shiphrah and Puah brought—in for questioning. "What have you done?" said King Pharaoh. The women responded, "The Hebrew women aren't like the Egyptian women; they're vigorous. Before the midwife can get there, they've already had the baby."

Vigorous means strong willed and determined. In the above passage, the midwives told their leader that the strong, fit, and determined women pushed their babies out and gave birth before they could carry out the assignment to assassinate the male children. The King knew that the deliver would come from the womb of a woman. He knew that the Male child would carry the government upon His shoulders.

The midwives feared God not what man could do to them and so the King furious with what didn't take place sent a decree out for all male children that were two years old and under to be assassinated, thrown in the river. The wicked massacre ordered by Pharaoh caused many women to suffer great pain. The cries and weeps from the mothers could be heard for days. However, Pharaoh was unsuccessful in reaching the chosen one. God blocked the attempts of an attack that could have killed  what He called to deliver His people from out of bondage. Jesus survived, yes relocated from this place to that place, but he carried out the assignment of God's plan.

What God has divinely prepared to come forth from the womb with power, dominion, and authority shall produce greatness!

King Pharaoh was controlled by the spirit of Lucifer. Anything that has purpose assigned to it— the enemy sets out to destroy it in its earliest stage. Lucifer is the enemy to the seed of righteousness. Anyone born of God is created in His righteousness and the enemy knows that.  The enemy strategically sets out to rob, steal, and kill our preordained purpose. However, he is already defeated.

Many times, the enemy tried to assassinate you before your purpose could ever come to fruition. There are many ways to kill a person. Most often, we relate it to being physically assaulted—

even if it is emotional or mental abuse. Many have suffered near death situations at the hands of an abuser. Most often, sexual abuse starts at an early age. It starts at a time when the child is vulnerable and unable to defend his or herself.

There's also emotional abuse—that which cuts deep into the core of your very soul? What about mental mind games, illness that causes schizophrenia, bipolar disorder, or impulsivity? The spirit of Pharaoh attempts to kill that which God has placed inside of you for the Kingdom. However you cannot die before you walk yoGods purpose for your life. Divine destiny awaits you. Abuse, dysfunction, and addiction cannot stop what God has placed a stamp of approval upon.

Today, be determined to press forward, reaching, and stretching toward the mark of that which you're passionate, sincere, and determined about. God has woven greatness in you so that you shall sit amongst great men and women. Yes, you will encounter the obstacles of life, but God has gone before you. He's made the crooked pathways straight. The weapon of Pharaoh shall form; however, it shall not prosper against you!

God has you in the palms of His hands. Nothing and no one will be able to pluck, pull, or pick you out! Walk into your destiny with the mentality that "all of my help comes from the Lord!"

# Destiny Step # 9:
# On your mark. Get ready. Get set. GO!

Therefore, since we also have a large cloud of witnesses surrounding us, let us lay aside every weight, and the sin that so easily ensnares us, and run with endurance the race that lies before us, keeping our eyes on Jesus, the author and the finisher of our faith.

Think back to the people in the book of Numbers. They finally broke camp. It may have taken several days to get ready. But, finally, the two silver trumpets sounded and the call was heard: "Rise up, O LORD! May your enemies be scattered; may your foes flee before you." (Numbers 10:35)

It was a short trip—they encamped on the banks of the Jordan and peered across the flooded river in the gathering dusk toward the city of Jericho.

Joshua, after a three day wait, instructed the people to consecrate themselves for the journey that was ahead. Joshua called a fast that would position them to endure the race that was set before them.

A promise will always come with preparation and principles attached to it. The vision that is being written and prepared now is for an appointed time later. You must be determined to remain face down and focused on that which God has given you.

The mission is to get over every obstacle, by any means necessary, and to lay aside the weights that attempt to hinder the progress of crossing over to the other side. Consecration is the process of cleaning oneself from the weight of old and unwanted filth that has attached itself to your heart, mind, body, and soul.

The weight of unneeded, outdated baggage can be a blessing blocker. One should not hold onto anything that is out to weigh them down. This slows up the process of reaching the other side. Consecrating allows you to be moved by the Spirit of God, and not by your flesh. Remember that nothing good is within our flesh.

In order to successfully crossover and walk into your destiny, the step of consecration must become a priority in your life. Consecration must become a lifestyle that is consistently practiced.

I have been told that, if you do something for 21 days—it then becomes a habit for you. If there is any validity to that, I suggest that you take the challenge. Rid yourself of that which you think you can't live without for 21 days. This might include things like certain foods, television shows, or social media. Replace these with spiritual things such as studying the Bible, praying more earnestly, and serving in your community.

The crossover will warrant consistent communication with God through prayer. Spending quality time with God in daily devotion and consecration will equip you with an ear to hear what the Spirit is saying.

Scripture says, "The sons and daughters of God will be moved by the spirit, not the flesh." Also, God says, "His sheep know His voice." Consecration allows you to be in tune with the spirit of God.

Everybody has things in their lives that weigh them down. Everyone has situations in their life that prevent them from soaring, loving themselves, and living life the way God intended.

Have you ever noticed that the reason birds can fly high is because they are light? The Scripture informs us to lay aside every weight and sin that so easily besets us. Rid yourself of everything that hinders you from moving forward. This includes any person that tends to pull you down.

God has given you the GO to let go. Move forward—equipped with the mindset that you are well able to obtain the land. You shall receive the promise. A mind that is steadfast, unmovable, and certain in that which God has declared for your life will give you the victory.

We must set our minds on the things of God in order to effectively move forward into our destiny. Our perspective is not to focus on the problems that are before us, but to focus on the promise.

The Word of the Lord says to rise up, assume the position, and aim higher. He is increasing the size, volume, and level for you to possess the land. Consecrate! It's time to crossover into the new thing.

"Behold, I will do a new thing; now it shall spring forth; shall ye not know it? I will even make a way in the wilderness, and rivers in the desert. (Isaiah 43:19)

# Destiny Step #10: Love conquers all!

**Love the Lord your God with all of your heart, and with all your soul and with all your might, and to love your neighbor as you love yourselves." (Matthew 22:37)**

The greatest commandment, which includes a promise, is to love! In John 3:16, we read that "God so loved the world that He gave his only begotten Son, so that whosoever will call on the Lord shall be saved." God showed us that, when love was released, all human kind had the opportunity to experience healing, deliverance, peace, and of course—eternal life.

As we go throughout this life and encounter people from all nationalities, creed, color, and culture; we must express the love of God. Without love, the Word of the Lord says, "We are tinkling, sounding symbols making a lot of noise." Yes, we will encounter folk that will get on our last nerve, however, always remember that love will cover a multitude of sins. (1 Peter 4:8)

For many people, all that they need is a kind word, a pat on the back, or a love hug. To effectively move forward into our destiny, we must adopt a "love walk." In the book of 1 Samuel chapter 4, Saul set out with his army to find and kill David. At one point, Saul went into a cave for a bathroom break. David and his army of men were hiding in the same cave. David could have very well taken Saul out. Love wouldn't let him take matters into his own hands, though.

In other words, love will always overrule hate. It is not for the children of God to seek revenge.

God says that *vengeance belongs to the Lord.* As you take destiny steps into new territory, and into places that you've never occupied before, it will be the response of a soft answer that will turn away wrath. The love that you show to that person will give you ability to win them over to Christ! We will encounter people that are bitter, or angry with the way life has treated them, however we must follow peace with all man... and if it be in you, promote peace, love and harmony." I'm reminded of the Biblical story in the book of Ruth. It was love that kept Ruth connected to Naomi. She spoke to Naomi from her heart saying, "Where you go, I will go, and your God will be my God!" That's the heart of a true friend. That's the heart of a person that will stick it out with you through whatever obstacle this life brings. God weighs the motives and intentions of our heart. The heart is the core of our being! ....God says, "above all else guard your heart, out of it flows the issues of life"!

Love, of course, keeps no record of any wrong. Love suffers long, love forgives, love prefers others over oneself, loves sees the needs of another and serves accordingly.

# Destiny Step #11: Speak Life

**"Death and life are in the power of the tongue:
and they that love it shall eat the fruit thereof.
(Proverbs 18:21)**

In the book of Exodus, chapter 17, Moses and the Israelites were camped in Rephidim. The Israelites had been traveling for some time and became thirsty. However, there was no place in sight to get water. The people became very angry with Moses. Moses cried out to the Lord for help.

Having heard the cry of Moses, God instructed him to use his staff to strike a rock. In doing so, water came flowing forth out of the rock. Knowing that God hadn't failed him yet, Moses was obedient to that which God told him to do. The water came forth and all the people witnessed the power of God's spoken word. The lesson to be learned from this story is to do exactly what God instructs us to do when He tells us to do it. When God speak to a situation, being obedient to His command will bring forth the miracles.

Fast forward to the book of Numbers 20:1-13, where Moses and his people continued on their journey. They arrived at the Desert of Zin and the people again became thirsty. They argued with Moses and Aaron saying, "If only we had died back in bondage. Why did you bring us out here where there is no water to drink?"

The response from a people that God set free was unbelievable! God reveals that, in spite of the miracles he performed in the presence of the people, their mindset was still in bondage! My God! We can have all the information in the world needed to propel us further on our journey, however, if we don't believe and have faith, then we just have information hanging in the wind.

When the people cried out to God for water, Moses was obedient to a degree, but we must not forget the other side of the story. Moses and Aaron went to the Lord and laid prostrate in prayer. God showed up with these words, "Take the staff and you and your brother bring all the people together."

He continued, "*Speak* to the rock before their eyes and it will pour out its water. You will bring water out of the rock for the people and their livestock." However, Moses didn't do what God told him to do. Moses instead took matters into his own hands and *struck* the rock. Water did come forth from the rock; however, the disobedience of Moses caused him to be banned from going into the Promised Land. Moses was only allowed to view the Promised Land from a distance. Can you imagine being at the promised place, but never stepping into it because of your desire to please ungrateful people? (Deuteronomy 32:49)

It would be shameful to have worked so hard to reach a destination and, because of disobedience, not able to occupy the land.

Stepping into Destiny will require us to do exactly what God has given us to do. If He says *go right*, don't' follow your instinct, flesh, or other people. Head in the direction He instructed you to go. Speak what God has ordered and ordained and, in doing so, you shall see the manifested glory of God. His word is a seed and, when we release it into the earth, we shall receive a harvest of God's glory. Life will happen to us all. How we respond to our situations and unfavorable circumstances will determine if the glory of God will be revealed. In the book of Hebrews, the writer tells us that, "God's word is living, active, and convicting." The Word of God is able to penetrate to the heart, bones, and marrow of a person. In other words, the Word of God goes deep so that growth, healing, and deliverance takes place.

When Moses spoke the word, it changed the atmosphere and attitude of the naysayers that said it couldn't happen. The word did just what it set out to do, producing a miracle. God will bless you with an abundant return as you take destiny steps—declaring and decreeing his word. A step of destiny requires the release of your faith. Faith is the substance of things hoped for and the evidence of things not seen. We must recite the promise of God on a daily basis. As the promise is spoken into the atmosphere, you must believe that God's word will not return unto Him void. Speak into the atmosphere, so that every good and perfect gift shall come from above. Speaking His word will manifest amazing power. Divine destiny steps will require you to be placed front and center into a lifeless situation. Let's take a look at the story of Ezekiel.

In the book of Ezekiel, chapter 37, Ezekiel begins his account with these words: "The hand of the Lord was upon me and carried me out in the spirit of the Lord and set me down in the midst of the valley which was full of dry bones." Now, if a dog were to be placed in the field where Ezekiel stood, it would have been doggy heaven. However, Ezekiel was knee deep in dry corpses. It was obvious that there was a plan and God would bring about an expected end.

Picture the scene for a moment. Ezekiel is standing in a place filled with dry and decayed bodies. Bones of small and large stature—hip bones, knee bones, and face bones laying at his feet. In the midst of a multitude of brittle and broken bones, Ezekiel is told to speak God's word. It would be most difficult to speak to a dead audience but when God chooses you to perform a thing, He anoints you to do it. We are reminded that the place where Ezekiel stood was Sodom and Gomorrah. A place filled with wickedness. A place that, at one time, was up, alive and popping. Everything wicked that could take place under the sun happened right where Ezekiel was standing. This situation looked completely hopeless, however, these dry bones had purpose attached to them. God knew the bones represented a people that he had a plan for. The bones represented a people that did not have a relationship with God. Scripture tells us that "he that has the Son has life; and he that hath not the Son of God has no life." (1 John 5:12)

Spiritually speaking, he who has no life is deemed as good as dead. Destiny steps will position you to speak God's word over lifeless, dry souls. This will bring about new life. You must speak words that will revive the soul, as well as the dry bones of people that are controlled by a life of sin. In the book of Proverbs chapter 15:4, Scripture reads, "A wholesome tongue is a tree of life: but perverseness therein is a breach in the spirit." Remember to speak life; you have the power within you. Jesus told his disciples, "Greater things will you do!" The vision within you must be stirred up. Dry souls are waiting upon your arrival! When God brings you to it, He will give you the power to do it. The wounded, the broken, *the least of these* are waiting on the words that will come out of your mouth. There is victory in the words you and I decree, declare and believe! "Then God shall establish it. Step into your destiny!

# Destiny Step #12:
# Delayed but not denied!

**"Then said Martha unto Jesus, Lord, if you had been here, my brother would not have died".**
**(John 11:21)**

In the book of John chapter 11, Lazarus—a man that Jesus called his friend—suddenly passed away. When Jesus heard the news about Lazarus, He shed tears. Four days after Lazarus's death, Jesus went to visit where they laid his body. Jesus was greeted by Lazarus's sisters who spoke these painful words, "If you were here, Lazarus wouldn't have died!" Jesus was, perhaps, taken by surprise. He may have felt like they were accusing him of causing Lazarus's death. Nevertheless, Jesus responded, "This sickness is not unto death, but that God might be glorified!" Of course, at the time, they didn't understand what Jesus meant. Still, they knew what He said had purpose.

In this story, Jesus had assured the sisters that Lazarus's sickness was not unto death. Yes, he experienced a moment of separation. Yes, the wrappings of a mere man were upon him. Yes, he was thrown in the tomb amongst the dust and darkness of the world. However, Lazarus had a promise attached to his life—no matter what invaded his mind, body, and spirit. All that Lazarus had gone through was just a set up for a testimony to those that discoUnited him. But God revealed to his haters that even death has to give back what God created for greater. Amen! Jesus instructed the same folk that wrapped Lazarus up to unwrap him. See, in your life, people have placed you in the grave. They assumed that there was no hope for you, so they wrapped you up with negative words and showed you ill behavior. Perhaps—because you were a high school dropout, or you were a teenage mom, or you were raised in the projects—people have mistreated you. People mistreated you by hurling words of insult and wrapping you up with unwanted words that were intended to keep you bowed down and bent over. Lazarus had a friend in Jesus. A friend that had enough compassion upon him that he decreed to his haters to lose him and let him go! So don't fret because of evildoers. Stay humble while on this journey to divine destiny. Despite the foolishness of folks, decide to shake it off. Be the better person because, in due season, God will exalt you to the place that He has planned for you!

For many of us, it was only when we had an encounter with God that the wrappings of man fell off of us! We heard the voice of our Creator calling to arise and come forth. What a mighty God we serve! Lazarus's destiny, at that season in his life, was to experience a dying in the flesh so that his spirit would arise and take its rightful position on the road to its final destination. A transformation of death to life took place right in the presence of his family, friends, and the enemy! God wasn't taken by surprise by what happened. Lazarus was a witness to the awesome power of God which declares "all things are possible to them that believe." The Lord revealed that He is the God of the impossible.

If God said it—that settles it. His word is just what it declares: "Sharper than any two-edged sword cutting everything in its way down to the bone and marrow." The Word of God is the light that will shine in the midst of the darkness. It provides grace for all guilt and shame. It is the joy for all sorrow. It is hope to the hopeless. It is life to a dying world. It is a savior for the sin-sick soul. It provides the overcoming power to defeat the lies of the enemy. His word is healing for the hurting. It binds up the broken hearted. It opens up the blind eyes and it declares the acceptable year of the Lord.

"In the beginning was the Word, and the Word was with God, and the Word was God... and the Word became flesh." (John 1:1, 14)

Jesus Christ is God's only begotten Son. Just as God was faithful and stayed with Jesus, He will never leave or forsake you. He will be with you as you step into your destiny!

"Now faith is the substance of things hoped for, the evidence of things not seen." (Hebrews 11:1)

Scripture tells us in Matthew 17:20 that—if we have faith the size of a mustard seed—it will equip us with the power to move mountains. I believe Jesus is implying that a small mustard seed of faith will cause whatever unwanted, unfavorable, or unacceptable situations are in your life to be removed. We could never possess the physical strength needed to literally pick a mountain up and relocate it to another destination. God uses this illustration to demonstrate how powerful a small mustard seed of faith can be.

One of Jesus's disciples, Peter, walked on water because of one word from Jesus: "Come." Peter, out of all the other disciples, moved with faith because he believed that, if God spoke it, so shall it be. At times, on your journey to divine destiny, you will be challenged to trust in God—even when it looks impossible. He may just speak one word into your situation, causing you to have faith that is rooted and grounded. You must have the kind of faith that believes God said it and it shall be; despite what stands before you. God is able to do the impossible!

The enemy almost always magnifies a situation to be larger than what it is. This is a strategic plan to bind up our faith and to setup doubt. The enemy knows that a cluttered mind cannot think on what God has already given you the victory over. If we would just think back on the situations that God showed up in, we would remember and declare this—since God did it before, surely, he will do it again. Never allow the enemy to distort your remembrances. Whatever the situation you face, it's probably a situation that you've seen before. The enemy doesn't want you to be reminded of your history with Heaven. God opened the Heavens before; pouring you out the blessing that was needed. Will He not hear your cry this time and do it again? Remember that God is with you as you step out on faith. Faith in God's plan equips you to triumphantly and victoriously move forward into your destiny.

Destiny steps empower you to step out on faith. All too often, because of fear, we stay close to the shoreline when God is calling for us to launch out into the deep. Casting your net close to the shore may allow you to catch a few fish. However—

the further out you go, the greater your chances of catching the abundance are.

Remember that God is with you as you step out on faith. Having unshakable faith in God's plan for your life equips you with all that is necessary to triumphantly and victoriously move forward. Step into your destiny. Be mindful that your best days are ahead of you! You shall have what you decree..now Step!!.

# ABOUT THE AUTHOR

Evangelist Sherri Lynn Dunn was born and raised in Louisville, KY. She is a licensed minister with Christ Temple Christian Life Center and a graduate of National College of Business and Technology. She has studied psychology at Spalding University and counseling at Campbellsville University. Evangelist Dunn started doing outreach ministry—reaching the wounded, brokenhearted, addicted, abandoned, abused, and homeless with the love of Jesus Christ. Dunn is the host of "His View," a local television show that airs every Saturday. She has led countless people to Jesus through preaching the gospel.

# REFERENCES

Scriptures referenced from the NIV and King
James Version of the Bible.

Made in the USA
Monee, IL
05 January 2022